Why Educational Policies Can Fail

An Overview of Selected African Experiences

World Bank Discussion Papers
Africa Technical Department Series

Studies on Implementation of African Educational Policies

No. 82   *Why Educational Policies Can Fail: An Overview of Selected African Experiences*

No. 83   *Comparative African Experiences in Implementing Educational Policies*

No. 84   *Implementing Educational Policies in Ethiopia*

No. 85   *Implementing Educational Policies in Kenya*

No. 86   *Implementing Educational Policies in Tanzania*

No. 87   *Implementing Educational Policies in Lesotho*

No. 88   *Implementing Educational Policies in Swaziland*

No. 89   *Implementing Educational Policies in Uganda*

No. 90   *Implementing Educational Policies in Zambia*

No. 91   *Implementing Educational Policies in Zimbabwe*

The set of studies on implementation of African educational policies was edited by Mr. George Psacharopoulos. Mr. Psacharopoulos wishes to acknowledge the help of Professor G. Eshiwani, who beyond being the author of the case study on Kenya (see No. 85) has coordinated the production of the other case studies in the region.

82

World Bank Discussion Papers
Africa Technical Department Series

Why Educational Policies Can Fail

An Overview of Selected African Experiences

George Psacharopoulos

The World Bank
Washington, D.C.

Copyright © 1990
The International Bank for Reconstruction
and Development/THE WORLD BANK
1818 H Street, N.W.
Washington, D.C. 20433, U.S.A.

All rights reserved
Manufactured in the United States of America
First printing July 1990

Discussion Papers present results of country analysis or research that is circulated to encourage discussion and comment within the development community. To present these results with the least possible delay, the typescript of this paper has not been prepared in accordance with the procedures appropriate to formal printed texts, and the World Bank accepts no responsibility for errors.

The findings, interpretations, and conclusions expressed in this paper are entirely those of the author(s) and should not be attributed in any manner to the World Bank, to its affiliated organizations, or to members of its Board of Executive Directors or the countries they represent. The World Bank does not guarantee the accuracy of the data included in this publication and accepts no responsibility whatsoever for any consequence of their use. Any maps that accompany the text have been prepared solely for the convenience of readers; the designations and presentation of material in them do not imply the expression of any opinion whatsoever on the part of the World Bank, its affiliates, or its Board or member countries concerning the legal status of any country, territory, city, or area or of the authorities thereof or concerning the delimitation of its boundaries or its national affiliation.

The material in this publication is copyrighted. Requests for permission to reproduce portions of it should be sent to Director, Publications Department, at the address shown in the copyright notice above. The World Bank encourages dissemination of its work and will normally give permission promptly and, when the reproduction is for noncommercial purposes, without asking a fee. Permission to photocopy portions for classroom use is not required, though notification of such use having been made will be appreciated.

The complete backlist of publications from the World Bank is shown in the annual *Index of Publications,* which contains an alphabetical title list (with full ordering information) and indexes of subjects, authors, and countries and regions. The latest edition is available free of charge from the Publications Sales Unit, Department F, The World Bank, 1818 H Street, N.W., Washington, D.C. 20433, U.S.A., or from Publications, The World Bank, 66, avenue d'Iéna, 75116 Paris, France.

ISSN: 0259-210X

George Psacharopoulos is chief of the Human Resources Division in the Latin America and the Caribbean Technical Department of the World Bank.

Library of Congress Cataloging-in-Publication Data

Psacharopoulos, George.
    Why educational policies can fail: an overview of selected
African experiences / George Psacharopoulos
      p. cm.—(Studies on implementation of African educational
policies, ISSN 0259-210X)   (World Bank discussion papers ;
82. Africa Technical Department series)
   Includes bibliographical references.
   ISBN 0-8213-1549-8
   1. Education and state—Africa—Case studies.   2. Comparative
education.   I. Title.   II. Series.   III. Series: World Bank
discussion papers ; no. 82.   IV. Series: World Bank discussion
papers. Africa Technical Department series.
LC95.A2P75   1990
379.6—dc20   90-40069
                                                                                                           CIP

FOREWORD

The decades of the 1960s and 1970s witnessed dramatic quantitative growth in African education systems. Beyond expanding educational places, many African countries pronounced intentions to "reform" their educational systems, by adjusting the length of education cycles, altering the terms of access to educational opportunity, changing the curriculum content, or otherwise attempting to link the provision of education and training more closely to perceived requirements for national socio-economic development. Strong economic growth performances of most African economies encouraged optimistic perceptions of the ability of governments to fulfill educational aspirations which were set forth in educational policy pronouncements.

Sadly, the adverse economic conditions of the 1980s, combined with population growth rates which are among the highest in the world meant that by the early 1980s, education enrollment growth stalled and the quality of education at all levels was widely regarded as having deteriorated. In recognition of the emerging crisis in African education, the World Bank undertook a major review to diagnose the problems of erosion of quality and stagnation of enrollments. Emerging from that work was a policy study, Education in Sub-Saharan Africa: Policies for Adjustment, Revitalization, and Expansion, which was issued in 1988. That study does not prescribe one set of education policies for all of Sub-Saharan Africa. Rather, it presents a framework within which countries may formulate strategies tailored to their own needs and circumstances. In fact, a central point which is stressed in the study is the need for each country to develop its own country-specific education strategy and policies, taking into account the country's unique circumstances, resource endowment and national cultural heritage.

The crucial role of national strategies and policies cannot be over-emphasized. In recognition of the centrality of sound policies as a basis for progress, in 1987 the Bank's Education and Training Department (the relevant unit responsible for the policy, planning and research function at that time) commissioned a set of papers by African analysts on the comparative experiences of eight Anglophone Eastern and Southern African countries, each of which had developed and issued major education policy reforms or pronouncements. The papers give special attention to deficiencies in the design and/or implementation processes that account for the often-yawning gaps between policy intentions and outcomes. The lessons afforded by the eight African case studies, along with a broader-perspective assessment of educational policy implementation, are presented in the papers by George Psacharopoulos (the overall manager of the set of studies) and John Craig. The eight country case studies are presented in companion reports.

By disseminating this set of studies on the implementation of African educational policies, it is hoped that the lessons of experience will be incorporated into the current efforts by African countries to design and implement national policies and programs to adjust, revitalize and selectively expand the education and training systems which prepare Africa's human resources, the true cornerstone of African development.

Hans Wyss
Director
Technical Department
Africa Region

ABSTRACT

The paper reviews a number of educational policy statements in East African countries, on issues ranging from combining education with production at the primary level to the financing of higher education. An assessment is made as to how successful the policies have been in achieving their original intention. The paper's conclusion is that policy outcomes fall far short of matching expectations, mainly because of insufficient, or the absence of, implementation. The reason most educational policies are not implemented is that they are vaguely stated and the financing implications are not always worked out. Another reason for failure is that the content of a policy is based on an empirically unsustained theoretical relationship between instruments and outcomes. The paper makes a plea for the formulation of more concrete, feasible and implementable policies based on documented cause-effect relationships.

ACKNOWLEDGEMENTS

Beyond being the author of the Kenya case study (see Discussion Paper Number 85), Professor S. Eshiwani has coordinated the production of the other case studies in the region. Ana Maria Arriagada has assisted in the compilation of the background material in this part of the present study.

TABLE OF CONTENTS

1. INTRODUCTION..1

2. THE POLICIES..2

    <u>Primary Education Policies</u>...3
    Increased Coverage..3
    Quality Improvement...4
    Combining Education with Production...6
    <u>Secondary Education Policies</u>...7
    Curriculum Diversification..8
    Better Links to Employment..9
    <u>Vocational Educational Policies</u>...10
    <u>Higher Education Policies</u>...11
    <u>Other Policies</u>..12
    National Unity...12
    Political Ideology...12
    Financing..12
    Regulation...15

3. COMPARATIVE LESSONS..16

4. CONCLUDING REMARKS...21

    BIBLIOGRAPHY...22

1. INTRODUCTION

"Educational policy" is perhaps the contemporary equivalent of what twenty years ago was known as "educational planning." Whatever it is, and no matter how many other disguises it takes (such as "educational reform"), practically every country in the world has at one time or another proclaimed the intention of making decisions that affect some aspect of schooling in society. It is in this wider sense that the term educational policy is used in this essay.

Of course educational policy is proclaimed or a school reform is enacted, not for their own sake, but in order to serve a particular purpose. The purpose can be pedagogical, political, economic, or any combination of other good causes according to the judgement of that impersonal entity often referred to as "the policy maker."

What has been the record of educational policy making in developing countries? Were intended reforms implemented in the first place, and if they were, did they have their expected effect? If not, why not? This paper attempts to give an answer to such complex questions by concentrating on one world region, Africa, and on a handful of typical attempted reforms that span the full educational ladder.

2. THE POLICIES

Educational policy statements are found in a variety of official documents such as:

a) Political statements or manifestos, e.g., Nyerere's most famous <u>Education for Self Reliance</u>, The Workers Party of Ethiopia <u>Programme</u>, or Swaziland's <u>Imbokodvo National Manifesto</u>;

b) Reports of special commissions, e.g., Zambia's "Lockwood Report," or Ethiopia's 1971 <u>Education Sector Review</u>;

c) The country's educational plan, often embedded in the country's Development Plan, e.g., <u>Education</u>, in Botswana's <u>National Development Plan 1979-85</u>,[1] or Uganda's <u>Ten Year Development Plan, 1981-1990</u>;

d) Ministry of Education Acts, Orders or Circulars, e.g., Lesotho's "National University Act, 1975.";

e) Reports of international agencies, e.g., UNESCO's 1961 <u>Outline of a Plan for African Educational Development</u> (better known as the "Addis Ababa Conference").

Policy statements in the above documents typically refer to the following:

a) Primary Education: Increasing coverage, improving teaching quality, combining education with production, teaching in local languages;

b) Secondary Education: Increasing coverage, diversifying the curriculum, improving links with employment;

c) Vocational Education: Meeting manpower requirements, providing the skills needed by a modernizing economy;

---

[1] pp. 99-132

d) Higher Education: Indigenizing higher civil service, meeting high level manpower needs;

e) Overall: Promoting cultural needs, serving political ideology, education financing and system regulation.

Let us follow the above taxonomy and document for a number of countries the exact formulation of policies, as stated in the official documents and, where possible, the outcome of such policies.

Primary Education Policies

Increased Coverage

Such policy intention is encountered in practically every country in the region, from independence to date. For example, one resolution of the Addis Ababa Conference was that "All African States" should aim at achieving universal primary education (UPE) within a maximum of 20 years."[2] In Swaziland, "The ultimate goal is to achieve universal free primary education for every child."[3] In Lesotho, "Every ... Mosotho child should complete a seven-year primary course."[4]

Although the Addis Ababa conference proposed a 71 percent participation rate in primary education by 1971, by 1974 Ethiopia had only achieved a rate of 18 percent.[5] An attempt in Ethiopia to set less ambitious targets for the expansion of primary education -- the Minimum Formation Education, a result of the 1972 Education Sector Review -- which could last as little as one year and be terminal for most students, was rejected, mainly by the teachers. According to some, it has contributed to the 1974 revolution.[6] Also in Ethiopia, a

---

[2] Unesco, 1961b, p.10
[3] Manifesto, 1972
[4] Lesotho, Education Sector Survey Report, 1982, paragraph 5.1
[5] Kiros, 1990
[6] ibid.

major Literacy Campaign was launched in 1979 to eradicate illiteracy by 1987. Today, the illiteracy rate in Ethiopia is on the order of 45 percent.[7]

In Zambia, the 1962 National United Independence Party's (UNIP) "Educational Manifesto" promised compulsory primary education up to the age of 15. Although, considerable progress was made over the next two decades in terms of increased coverage, the 1985 UNIP's "Policies for the Decade 1985-95" reemphasized compulsory, but not free education to grade 9 (i.e. to the end of junior secondary).[8]

In Uganda, the situation today is one of "increasing illiteracy."[9] And in Lesotho, "... although access to primary education is open to all, UPE has not been achieved."[10]

Rapid population growth is often blamed for the non-implementation of UPE in African countries. In Zambia, for example, when UPE was espoused in the early sixties the population growth rate was of the order of 2 percent. By 1985 it stood at 3.4 percent. "If ... the Zambian government insists on its goal of universal basic education (grades 1-9) for all, 1.74 million additional school places would have to be added to the current 1.3. million by the year 2000. ... This is clearly a daunting task given that education will have to compete with other social services for increasingly dwindling national revenues."[11]

Quality Improvement

Of course, beyond coverage, many African states set a goal to improve the quality of education children receive. Emphasis has been on: teacher training, construction of schools, student/teacher ratio. For example, in Zambia's First Development Plan (1966-70) the objective was to improve primary education by means of expanding teacher training.[12]

---

[7]UNESCO, 1985
[8]Achola, 1990
[9]Odaet, 1990
[10]Thelehani, 1990
[11]Achola, 1990
[12]ibid.

The 1963 Report of the Uganda Education Commission (paragraph 27) stated that "The task... is not just to provide more primary schools but to provide better primary education". Yet in Uganda today there is a "high dropout rate at almost every level of the educational system.[13] "Training Colleges should be filled to capacity."[14] "Teachers' salaries must not be allowed to fall below the general level of salaries... to arrest the drift into other occupations."[15] "The raising of the teaching quality of Training Colleges is a high priority."[16]

In Swaziland, the Second Development Plan (1972-1978) set the objective "to raise the quality of education by reducing the high incidence of dropout and repeaters."[17] One way to do this, was to reduce the student-teacher ratio from 45:1 to 36:1 within the planning period. This indeed happened, although none of the expected effects followed: "Despite the reduction in the pupil-teacher ratio... instead of the normal 7 years to produce a primary school graduate, it took 12.6 years in 1981... The number of repeaters went up over the plan period... by nearly 50 percent... There was no improvement in the overall pass rate SPCE during the plan period (Swaziland Primary Certificate Examination)."[18]

In Lesotho, "In spite of... programs... geared to produce large numbers of teachers.... there is a chronic shortage of teachers... worse in the sciences. The latest is the brain drain in South Africa where salaries are very high."[19] "The pushout rate is high. Only 14 percent of primary school graduates enter secondary education." Also, "... there is an apparent decline in the quality of education, like bad examination results."[20]

---

[13] Odaet, 1990
[14] Uganda Education Commission, 1963, paragraph 142
[15] Kenya Ministry of Education, 1964, paragraph 549
[16] Uganda Education Commission, Report of the National Committee on Education, 1963, paragraph 143-144
[17] cited by Magagula, 1990
[18] Magagula, 1990
[19] Telehani, 1990
[20] ibid.

After several years of emphasizing the improvement of the quality of education in Ethiopia, it is recognized that "... it has not been easy to raise the quality of education in a significant manner...."[21]

In Botswana, "... the quality of primary education has fallen short of people's expectations...."[22] In 1979 ...36% of [primary school] classes were without a classroom of their own."[23]

In Tanzania "there is a big shortage of teachers.... By April 1982, primary schools in the country had a shortage of 34.94 percent of the required number of teachers."[24]

Combining Education With Production

The impetus for such policy change came from the push for "relevance" in education. The Plan for Action [25] clearly stated "That the following measures be adopted for absorbing the surplus of unskilled manpower: (a) that primary education be given a practical bias."[26] But in Tanzania, pursuant to Education for Self-Reliance, the Third Five Year Development Plan states that "Work is to be more integrated with theoretical subjects."[27]

In Zimbabwe the Government also adopted the philosophy of education with production "... to make school experiences meaningful and worthwhile in terms of real life activities outside the school campus."[28] But "The problem... was that most of the teachers did not understand the philosophy of education with production.... Rather they saw it in terms of... activities associated with

---

[21] The Workers Party of Ethiopia, Programme, 1979, p.96
[22] Botswana National Development Plan, 1980, p.99
[23] Botswana National Development Plan, 1985-91, p.126
[24] Tanzania Ministry of Education, 1984, p.12
[25] UNESCO, 1961b, p.21
[26] For at least two notable exceptions to this rule, the 1963 Uganda Education Commission (paragraph 47) states: "Agriculture is not a suitable subject for primary schools." Also in Kenya, "... we do not recommend the inclusion of a specifically vocational element in the primary course." (Kenya, Report of the National Committee on Educational Objectives and Policies, paragraph 27).
[27] Tanzania Ministry of Education, 1980, p. 24
[28] Mutumbuka, Education Minister, 1984, as cited by Maravanyika, 1986, p.27

vocationalism long rejected by Blacks during the colonial era.... The schools... failed to attract staff with the appropriate qualifications for meaningful practical skills teaching. To date, education with production is more of a slogan than a meaningful educational philosophy...."[29]

In Lesotho also, "The school system has definitely failed to produce... persons ready to be involved in rural and manual work...."[30] "Practical subjects are regarded by learners and parents as second rate in the educational scene. Incidentally, the introduction of practical subjects is an attempt to make education relevant."[31]

In Zambia, "... production training should be a compulsory subject which shall form an integral part of the curriculum."[32] "The president issued a decree that... all educational institutions would combine education with productive activity. The ... aims were to foster in pupils and students respect and love for manual work. The program has had only marginal impact on the students.... Academic education, which paves the way for entry into the university attracts the most able students and subsequently offers the best rewards in terms of social standing...."[33]

Secondary Education Policies

With some progress achieved in primary education, it was the next stage of education that naturally received attention: "The urgent need for expansion of secondary education is emphasized."[34] But in Swaziland, the government decided in 1975 that "secondary system expansion was to be determined by manpower requirements,"[35] and so did, earlier on, Tanzania. In all African countries, the expansion of secondary education had to be linked, one way or

---

[29] Maravanyika, 1990
[30] Thelejani, 1990
[31] ibid.
[32] Zambia Ministry of Education, 1977, chapter 8, paragraph 13
[33] Achola, 1990
[34] Uganda Education Commission, 1963, paragraph 58
[35] Magagula 1990

another, to the world of work. E.g. "Education will be made more relevant to the world of work...."[36]

Curriculum Diversification

This has been the equivalent of combining education with production at the secondary level: "To meet the demands of ...African social and economic life...is the need to expand the curriculum at the second level in the direction of more <u>technical and vocational education</u>. Such programmes are necessary to provide the skilled and semi-professional manpower essential for economic growth."[37] "The concept of 'secondary education' should be broadened to include practical training and to provide outlets into the production side of industry and agriculture."[38] All the existing trade schools should be closed or transformed into the new type of secondary school with a vocational bias."[39] "A Workshop...is a necessary part of the equipment of any secondary school...."[40]

In Tanzania, "secondary education vocationalization is to be realized so that each secondary school leaver will have a skill useful to the economy."[41] "The general aim of education is terminal and aims at equipping the pupils with skills...To achieve this, secondary education is diversified and vocationalized into commercial, technical, agricultural and home economics biases."[42] However, a recent evaluation of the diversification policy in Tanzania revealed that it failed to achieve the above objectives, e.g., one year after graduation in agriculture, only 12 percent of the agricultural bias graduates were employed in agriculture, and only 5 percent followed further

---

[36] Botswana National Development Plan, 1980, p.99
[37] UNESCO, 1961b, Addis Ababa Conference, chapter 1, p.6; emphasis in the original
[38] Kenya Ministry of Education, Report of the National Committee, 1964, paragraph 74
[39] Uganda Commission on Education, 1963, chapter VI
[40] Kenya, Report of the National Committee, paragraph 74
[41] Tanzania Ministry of Education, 1980, p.24
[42] Tanzania Ministry of Education, 1980, pp.3, 4

studies related to agriculture.[43] And "... many employers do not recognize the level of competence in skills acquired .. in the diversified schools."[44]

Also in Kenya, a tracer study in industrial school graduates did not reveal any employment advantage over a control group of academic secondary school graduates.[45]

Better Links to Employment

The Addis Ababa Plan for Action[46] recommended that the first step in the educational planning process should be "... an estimation of forward manpower requirements under the dual system of occupational and educational classification... undertaken by each country with the help of Unesco." Most countries followed the recommendation. E.g., in Kenya, "From the manpower figures we calculate a... requirement of Form I entries of 66,000..., but... believing that this is an underestimate... we approve to provide facilities for about 87,000 pupils...."[47]

Ethiopia introduced a system of comprehensive secondary schools in 1962 "designed to meet the...middle-level manpower demand in technical and commercial fields... [but] by 1969 the system was found to be defective... When tools stand idle for two to six years or more."[48] In spite of the manpower orientation of development plans in Ethiopia, as early as 1973 shortages and surpluses were reported for key occupations.[49] By 1981 the situation had become worse.[50]

In Uganda, also, in spite of a long tradition with manpower planning, there is a "widening gap between the educational programs offered in schools... and the actual openings available... in the employment market."[51] And in

---

[43]Psacharopoulos and Loxley, 1985, tables 6-35 and 6-37
[44]Tanzania Ministry of Education, 1984, p.23
[45]Narman and others 1984, table 3
[46]UNESCO, 1961b, p.22
[47]Kenya Education Commission, 1964, paragraphs 664-666
[48]Kiros, 1990
[49]ibid.
[50]ibid.
[51]Odaet, 1990

Botswana, "Manpower shortages persist, and the country remains over dependent on the skills of expatriates.[52]

It should be noted that fifteen years ago Jolly an Colclough (1972) surveyed over thirty manpower plans in Africa and concluded these "... manpower plans... inadequately served the planners." [53] Yet in many African countries today, such plans continue to be elaborated.

Vocational Education Policies

Vocationalism had a long tradition in Africa. The already mentioned 1961 recommendations of UNESCO's Plan for Action were echoed in the policy documents of many countries. In Swaziland, for example, "...the content of education must be work-oriented from the primary to the highest levels."[54] Also, Swaziland's Second Development Plan (1973-78) sets the objective "to reorient the curricula at both primary and secondary levels so as to... enable school leavers to move naturally into employment sectors."[55] "A permanent machinery should be established to ensure an adequate link between the supply and demand for trained manpower on the one hand, and to relate school curriculum to national employment prospects on the other. A comprehensive National Manpower Survey should be conducted to identify manpower requirements at all levels and feed back the information to the school system."[56]

In Zambia, "The main method of providing technical education in.. institutes under the Department of Technical Education and Vocational Training should be ...full-time pre-employment training in contrast to the apprenticeship method."[57]

In spite of such manpower orientation, unemployment is still very high in Africa today, while there are severe scarcities in some skills. In Zambia for

---

[52] Botswana National Development Plan, 1980, p. 99
[53] p. 254
[54] Swaziland Manifesto, 1972
[55] Magagula, 1990
[56] Swaziland National Education Review Commission as cited by Magugula
[57] Zambia Ministry of Education 1977, chapter 9, paragraph 4

example, "estimates range between 1 and 1.5 million unemployed.. school leavers. ... The government has responded by trying to popularize the agricultural sector.... The... efforts have, however, produced marginal success because of a strong negative attitude towards farming.... Distaste for manual work on the land is deeply rooted in Zambia...."[58] And in spite of the early emphasis on vocational secondary schools in Ethiopia, "many more students went to academic secondary schools... many more opportunities were offered in academic secondary schools than in vocational ones."[59] And "It is quite clear that the manpower planning exercise in Tanzania has been counterproductive, leading to a worsening of the fit between the supply of and demand for high- and medium-level workers...."[60]

Higher Education Policies

These have been dominated by attempts to meet high level manpower needs or to Africanize higher civil service. For example, "The ... University ... will be strengthened to meet future skilled manpower requirements in those disciplines for which the manpower study... shows it to be necessary."[61] Or, "To expand facilities for tertiary education in order to meet the manpower requirements of both public and private sectors,"[62] and "to provide technical skills through education and training to meet the high level manpower requirements for the economy."[63]

But in spite of such orientation, severe shortages are reported in some fields in Africa today, while there are surpluses in others.[64] And although Zambia has completed Zambianization almost completely within the administration, "the country has continued to rely on expatriates to fill many technical and professional jobs."[65]

---

[58]Achola, 1990
[59]Trudeau 1964, as cited by Kiros, 1986, p.36
[60]Cooksey, 1986, p.200
[61]Lesotho, Second Five Year Plan, 1975, para 7.22
[62]Swaziland Sectors Development Plan, 1973-78, as cited by Magagula 1986, p.17
[63]Uganda, 1981 Development Plan, paragraph 22.13m, (a)
[64]Hinchliffe, 1986
[65]Achola, 1990

Other Policies

Beyond the above set of policies referring to the respective levels of education, a host of other policies were formulated to serve various objectives that cut across levels.

National Unity

For example, "the purpose of education is to produce an enlightened and participant citizenry.... The policy...is that all education should ...inculcate love for the land, loyalty to King and country, self-respect, self-discipline, respect for the law accompanied by the highest degree of knowledge and the building of character."[66]

Also, teaching in local language has been a common policy for cultural unity, e.g. "Kiswahili should be the main vehicle for literacy work...."[67] Or, in Zambia, "... the widespread use of English as a medium of instruction... has promoted a sense of national unity.... The national motto of 'One Zambia, One Nation' could hardly make sense without a unifying language...."[68] But in Lesotho, "Officially the medium of instruction is Sesotho until the 4th grade.... In reality a mixture languages may go on.... This is partly blamed for the low standard in English...."[69]

Political Ideology

In Tanzania, soon after the Arushad Declaration on Socialism and Self-Reliance, Nyerere issued a major paper on Education for Self-Reliance (ESR). [For a superb analysis of ESR see Morrison, 1976, chapter 11.] This paper became the basis of all major educational changes in the country, implemented by the 1969 Education Act.[70] The 1974 Musoma Resolution urged "... that

---

[66] Kenya, Report of the National Committee, 1964, paragraph 104)
[67] Kenya, Report of the National Committee, 1964, paragraph. 104
[68] Achola 1990
[69] Telehani, 1990
[70] Tanzania Education Ministry of Education 1980, p.3

education be integrated with work," in order to develop "in each citizen ... an Ujamaa or socialist outlook."[71]

In Ethiopia, Proclamation No. 11 of 1974 setting out the objectives of the Development Campaign states as one of its objectives "to rid the people of self-seeking individualism and instill in them a spirit of cooperativeness for the common good."[72] "The Minister of Education shall... ensure that the educational curriculum is prepared on the basis of Hebrettesebawinet (socialism)."[73]

According to the Zimbabwe Minister of Education "The curriculum in our education system should be seen and considered as a vehicle towards the establishment of a socialist society."[74] Yet "... educational policies in Zimbabwe appear to be adversely influenced by an inherent dichotomy in the country's ideological orientation. On the one hand are the politicians bent on introducing Marxist-Leninist ideology which is unfamiliar to most people..., and on the other hand is the more ... entrenched capitalist infrastructure bequeathed by the colonial administration. This is more familiar and people are prepared to take a chance with it as they see others around them who have succeeded by it.... The majority of Blacks appear to be interested in the kind of education they had been denied than on something new and unfamiliar."[75]

Financing

Although every educational reform must have substantial financial implications, this issue is only rarely addressed. Or if it is addressed, it is relegated for further study or to third parties. For example, it is a mistake to think that the ambitious program set out in the 1961 UNESCO Addis Ababa Conference did not consider the financing aspect of the program. However, it delegated it to third parties. The conference: "Invites UNESCO to approach the competent international organizations, governments and public and

---

[71]Tanzania Ministry of Education 1980, p.3
[72]Negarit Gazeta, No. 10, 25 November 1974, p.41
[73]Negarit Gazeta, No. 29, 26 August 1977, article 11
[74]Mutumbuka 1984, as cited by Maravanyika, 1990
[75]Maravanyika, 1990

private institutions capable of providing large-scale assistance with the request that they contribute to the financing of such programs recommended by the African countries concerned."[76]

In the Plan for Action that followed the conference it was stated that, "It must be possible to finance both the recurring and non-recurring costs of education ... from loans as well as taxation.[77] And later, "That an increase in national education budgets requires use of new financial sources, both public and private, national and foreign, material and human."[78]

According to the Uganda Ten Year Development Plan, "An education tax will be introduced to augment the resource base of educational institutions.... Public, parastatal and private organizations will be encouraged to provide a training fund that will finance training...."[79]

It is interesting to note changes in the financing policy of schools, even within a few years. For example in Swaziland, the First Development Plan (1969-73) states that primary and secondary education should be free. In the Second (1973-78) Development Plan, however, the word "free" is dropped.[80] In Botswana, "... a proportion of the costs will be shared by the community...."[81]

In Tanzania, the 1982 Presidential Commission on Education watered down the earlier strict manpower forecasting criterion for the expansion of secondary education: "Both the 'Social Demand' and 'Manpower Needs' approaches will be used in development plans...."[82] "Parents of pupils attending secondary schools will now be required to contribute towards part of the cost for their children's education...."[83] Thus, in January 1985 a fee [of 1600 shillings per year] was imposed, which is equivalent to two months' salary of a clerk.

---

[76]UNESCO, 1961a, chapter 8, Resolution No. 1
[77]UNESCO, 1961b, p.10
[78]UNESCO 1961, Plan, p.20
[79]Uganda, Ten Year Reconstruction and Development Plan 1981-1990, 1981, paragraph 22.6
[80]Magagula, 1990
[81]Botswana, 1984
[82]Tanzania Ministry of Education 1984 p. 10
[83]Tanzania Ministry of Education, 1984, p. 17

Yet, in spite of such efforts, the financing of the recurrent cost of educational investment is the main constraint to further expansion or improvement of the system's quality in African countries, as well as elsewhere.[84]

Regulation

All African states have chosen to regulate non-government educational institutions in the name of quality control, equity or political ideology. For example, "The control of education lies with the government of Swaziland whether it concerns state schools, subsidized schools or private undertakings."[85] Or, "Independent technical and commercial colleges should be carefully controlled and high standards encouraged by a system of 'recognition as efficient.'"[86]

In 1975, the Provisional Military Administrative Council abolished private schools in Ethiopia at the stroke of a pen: "Private schools are hereby transferred to public ownership."[87]

Yet even in a socialist country like Tanzania, over 40 percent of the enrollment in secondary schools in 1979 was in private institutions.[88] In fact in Tanzania the share of secondary enrollments in private schools has nearly doubled between 1970 and 1983, 24 and 44 percent, respectively.[89]

---

[84]World Bank, 1986
[85]Imbokodvo Manifesto 1972
[86]Kenya, National Committee on Education, paragraph 111
[87]Negarit Gazeta, No. 3, 29 September 1975, p. 19
[88]Tanzania Ministry of Education 1980, 1979, p. 35
[89]Bellew, 1986, p.15

3. COMPARATIVE LESSONS

Are there any generalizations that can be drawn from the above examples of educational policy objectives and outcomes in a handful of African countries? Looking at the past record of educational policy making in Africa, (and possibly elsewhere), there are three main reasons why an intention or a reform may ex post not materialize or be seen as failure:

a) The intended policy was never implemented in the first place;

b) Even if an attempt at implementation was made, it failed to be completed or achieve a minimum critical mass so as to have an impact;

c) Although the policy was implemented, it did not have the intended effect.

Sub-reasons for failure within each of the above categories are as follows:

No implementation:

a) The policy intention was too vague, e.g. "the quality of education should be improved;"

b) The intention was lip service or a political statement, e.g., "there will be free education for all."

Partial implementation:

a) Neglect of a prerequisite factor, e.g., feasibility of financing;

b) Social rejection, e.g. vocational schools boycotted by parents.

Implementation but no effect:

a) Policy based on invalid theoretical model, e.g., basing educational expansion on manpower requirements;

b) Policy based on insufficient information/evidence, e.g. not knowing the exact number of teachers on the payroll in the first place.

Of course the definition of success or failure is a subjective matter. And the vague formulation of policy objectives makes evaluation even more difficult. To me, at least, announcing a policy and exciting people's expectations on an outcome that everyone knows at the outset is doomed, is a failure. To put it differently, impossibility of implementation, or even partial implementation, is a negative signal for the validity of any policy.

As an example let us revisit the report of the Conference of African States on the Development of Education in Africa [90] that set the following targets for the 1961-1980 period:

a) Primary education shall be universal, compulsory and free;

b) Education at the second level shall be provided to 30 percent of those who complete primary education;

c) Higher education shall be provided ... to 20 percent of those who complete secondary education;

d) The improvement of the quality of African schools and universities shall be a constant aim.

It does not take a thorough investigation to conclude that none of the good intentions put forward in this, and many other documents, have not been achieved. It is true that a lot of progress has been made in African education in the last twenty years, especially regarding increased coverage.[91] Yet the

---

[90] UNESCO 1961, p. 18
[91] Bellew, 1986

results are nowhere near the expectations. Table 1 shows how the Addis Adaba quantitative plans compare to the realizations.

Table 1

Enrollment Ratios in Africa: Planned versus Actual (percent)

Educational Level	Actual 1960	Planned 1980	Actual 1980	Actual vs. planned (shortfall)
	(1)	(2)	(3)	(4)
Primary	40	100	76	24
Secondary	3	23	16	30
Higher	0.2	2	1	50

Source: Cols. 1 and 2 from Unesco, 1961, p. 19, col. 3 from Bellew 1986, pp. 9-11
Col. 4 = [(Col. 2 - Col. 3)/Col. 2] x 100

The above averages of course hide the situation in individual countries, e.g., the primary enrollment ratio in the semi-arid low-income countries was only 28 percent in 1980, and 35 percent in Ethiopia in the same year.[92] Why such record? The degree of success or effect of a given policy is a product of two probabilities: that the policy has been implemented in the first place and, second, that it yields the intended effect:

POLICY EFFECT = PROB implementation x PROB effect

In at least one African country, "More has been achieved in enunciating new policy statements or in perfecting change in rhetoric than

---

[92]Bellew, 1986

in implementing or institutionalizing change."[93] This statement must apply to others since Craig (1986) in reviewing 153 educational policies in Sub-Saharan Africa, came to the conclusion that only a handful were implemented (Craig, Table 5). The rarely implemented policies mostly referred to educational expansion and the Harambee schools.

Table 2

The Record of Policy Implementation

Degree of Implementation	Number of cases	%
Unclear	28	18
None or little	113	74
Mostly	7	5
Fully	5	3
Total	153	100

Source: Craig, 1990

Of course there were moments of brilliance or pragmatism, but these are exceptions rather than the rule. For example, "The problems of agricultural education are not primarily educational, but are bound up with economic and social problems over which the Ministry of Education has no control."[94] Or, "some aspects of the educational reform would be implemented while others can only be implemented over a period of time, bearing in mind changing circumstances and constraints."[95] And rarely have

---

[93] Maravanyika, 1990
[94] Uganda Education Commission, 1963, paragraph 107
[95] Zambia, Ministry of Education 1977, chapter 17, paragraphs 2 and 3

performance criteria been set: "Successful agricultural education depends largely on visible evidence of successful farming."[96]

Most often, instead, there have been ambitious statements, such as: "Educational reforms should seek to improve quality without sacrificing quantity."[97] Or, "To provide increasing employment opportunities aimed at eliminating unemployment and underemployment in the country; and to insure absorption of trained manpower in appropriate positions."[98]

It is often said that educational reform alone is not possible without parallel transformations in society.[99] Yet countries that have adopted holistic social transformations, and placed education within such transformations (e.g. Tanzania since 1967 and Ethiopia since 1974) do not appear to have shown major success relative to other countries that have adopted in isolation some of the same policies. "Ethiopia was probably the first independent African country south of the Sahara to introduce comprehensive development planning... As the evidence has shown, there was little systematic effort made to translate plans into action."[100]

Unrealistic policies naturally lead to reversals, even within only one year. In Zambia, for example, in 1975 a radical educational reform was announced (Education for Development, 1976). In 1977, another document, Education Reform: Proposals and Recommendations, reversed the 1976 policies.[101]

---

[96]Uganda Education Commission, 1963, paragraph 114
[97]Zambia Ministry of Education, Educational Reform: Proposals and Recommendations, 1977, chapter 3, paragraph 2
[98]Uganda Development Plan, 1981, paragraph 22.13, b, c.
[99]Ergas, 1982
[100]Kiros 1990
[101]Lulat, 1982

4. CONCLUDING REMARKS

The above record gives a very pessimistic outlook regarding the success of educational reforms that are proposed today. In order to avoid past pitfalls, the following conditions should be met in formulating educational policies:

a) A policy statement should be <u>concrete</u> and <u>feasible</u> in terms of objectives, including a timetable, source of financing of its implementation, and institution responsible, e.g., "the net primary enrollment ratio in rural district X will increase from 30 to 50 percent by 1995, financed by a 2 percent tax on beer;"

b) The substance of a policy should be based on <u>research-proved</u> cause and effect relationships -- not goodwill or intuition. For example, this should exclude expanding the educational system according to manpower needs, or forcing students to enroll in types of schools and curricula for which the rewards in society are modest.

Unfortunately, concreteness cannot be easily observed in political statements, and the intuitive power of "I know what the country needs" is much stronger than whatever research results demonstrate. It is for this reason that ambitious but rarely implemented and non-effective policy statements, such as those in the above anthology, will continue to be with us in the foreseeable future. Perhaps the safest course of action for the policy maker would be to abstain from educational policy fireworks, and concentrate on the documentation of cause and effect relationships -- the only activity, in my opinion, that can lead to successful school reforms.

BIBLIOGRAPHY

Achola, P.P.W., — <u>Implementing Educational Policies in Zambia</u> World Bank Discussion Paper No. 90, The World Bank, 1990, Washington, D.C.

Bellew, R. — "African Education and Socioeconomic Indicators," World Bank Education and Training Division, Report No. EDT39, 1986

Botswana Ministry of Education — <u>Education through Partnership: Intermediate Schools of the Future</u>, 1984

Botswana Ministry of Finance and Development Planning — <u>National Development Plan 1979-85</u>, Gaborone, 1980

— <u>National Development Plan 1985-91</u>, Gaborone, 1984

Cooksey, B. — "Policy and Practice in Tanzanian Secondary Education Since 1967," <u>International Journal of Educational Development</u>, 6, No. 3, 1986, pp. 183-202

Craig, J.E. — <u>Comparative African Experiences in Implementing Educational Policies</u>, World Bank Discussion Paper Number 83, The World Bank, 1990, Washington, D.C.

Ergas, Z. — "Can Education be Used as a Tool to Build a Socialist in Africa? The Tanzanian Case," <u>Journal of Modern African Studies</u>, 20, 4, 1982: 571-594

Eshiwani, G. — <u>Implementing Educational Policies in Kenya</u>, World Bank Discussion Paper Number 85, The World Bank, Washington, D.C.

Ethiopia Government — <u>The Workers Party of Ethiopia: Programme</u>, Addis Ababa, 1979

Hinchliffe, K. — "Higher Education in Sub-Saharan Africa," Education and Training Department, The World Bank, 1986

Jolly, R. and Colclough, C. — "African Manpower Plans: An Evaluation," <u>International Labor Review</u>, 106-2-3, (August-September 1972), pp. 207-264

Kiros, F.G. — <u>Implementing Educational Policies in Ethiopia</u>, World Bank Discussion Paper Number 85, The World Bank, 1990, Washington, D.C.

Lulat, Y.G.M. — "Political Constraints on Educational Reform for Development: Lessons from an African Experience," <u>Comparative Education Review</u>, 26, June 1982, pp. 235-253

Magagula, C.	-	*Implementing Educational Policies in Swaziland*, World Bank Discussion Paper Number 91, The World Bank, 1990 Washington, D.C.
Maravanyika, O.E.	-	*Implementing Educational Policies in Zimbabwe*, World Bank Discussion Paper Number 91, The World Bank, Washington, D.C.
Morrison, D.R.	-	*Education and Politics in Africa: The Tanzanian Case*, Hurst & Co., 1976
Nyerere, J.	-	*Education for Self-Reliance*, Dar-es-Salaam, 1967
Odaet, C.F.	-	*Implementing Educational Policies in Uganda*, World Bank Discussion Paper Number 89, The World Bank, Washington, D.C.
Psacharopoulos, G. and Loxley, W.	-	*Diversified Secondary Education and Development: Evidence from Colombia and Tanzania*, Johns Hopkins University Press, 1985
Tanzania Ministry of Education	-	*Education System in Tanzania towards the Year 2000.* Dar-es-Saalam, 1984
	-	*Basic Facts about Education in Tanzania*, Dar-es-Saalam, 1980
Thelejani, T.S.	-	*African Educational Policies: Comparative Experiences -- Lesotho*, Education and Training Division, The World Bank, 1990
Trudeau, E.	-	*Higher Education in Ethiopia*, Montreal, 1964
UNESCO	-	*Final Report, Conference of African States on the Development of Education in Africa*, 1961a
	-	*Outline of a Plan for African Educational Development*, 1961b
	-	*Statistical Yearbook*, 1985
World Bank	-	*Financing Education in Developing Countries: An Exploration of Policy Options*, The World Bank, 1986

Distributors of World Bank Publications

ARGENTINA
Carlos Hirsch, SRL
Galeria Guemes
Florida 165, 4th Floor-Ofc. 453/465
1333 Buenos Aires

AUSTRALIA, PAPUA NEW GUINEA, FIJI, SOLOMON ISLANDS, VANUATU, AND WESTERN SAMOA
D.A. Books & Journals
648 Whitehorse Road
Mitcham 3132
Victoria

AUSTRIA
Gerold and Co.
Graben 31
A-1011 Wien

BAHRAIN
Bahrain Research and Consultancy Associates Ltd.
P.O. Box 22103
Manama Town 317

BANGLADESH
Micro Industries Development Assistance Society (MIDAS)
House 5, Road 16
Dhanmondi R/Area
Dhaka 1209

Branch offices:
156, Nur Ahmed Sarak
Chittagong 4000

76, K.D.A. Avenue
Kulna

BELGIUM
Publications des Nations Unies
Av. du Roi 202
1060 Brussels

BRAZIL
Publicacoes Tecnicas Internacionais Ltda.
Rua Peixoto Gomide, 209
01409 Sao Paulo, SP

CANADA
Le Diffuseur
C.P. 85, 1501B rue Ampère
Boucherville, Quebec
J4B 5E6

CHINA
China Financial & Economic Publishing House
8, Da Fo Si Dong Jie
Beijing

COLOMBIA
Enlace Ltda.
Apartado Aereo 34270
Bogota D.E.

COTE D'IVOIRE
Centre d'Edition et de Diffusion Africaines (CEDA)
04 B.P. 541
Abidjan 04 Plateau

CYPRUS
MEMRB Information Services
P.O. Box 2098
Nicosia

DENMARK
SamfundsLitteratur
Rosenoerns Allé 11
DK-1970 Frederiksberg C

DOMINICAN REPUBLIC
Editora Taller, C. por A.
Restauracion e Isabel la Catolica 309
Apartado Postal 2190
Santo Domingo

EL SALVADOR
Fusades
Avenida Manuel Enrique Araujo #3530
Edificio SISA, ler. Piso
San Salvador

EGYPT, ARAB REPUBLIC OF
Al Ahram
Al Galaa Street
Cairo

The Middle East Observer
8 Chawarbi Street
Cairo

FINLAND
Akateeminen Kirjakauppa
P.O. Box 128
SF-00101
Helsinki 10

FRANCE
World Bank Publications
66, avenue d'Iéna
75116 Paris

GERMANY, FEDERAL REPUBLIC OF
UNO-Verlag
Poppelsdorfer Allee 55
D-5300 Bonn 1

GREECE
KEME
24, Ippodamou Street Platia Plastiras
Athens-11635

GUATEMALA
Librerias Piedra Santa
Centro Cultural Piedra Santa
11 calle 6-50 zona 1
Guatemala City

HONG KONG, MACAO
Asia 2000 Ltd.
Mongkok Post Office
Bute Street No. 37
Mongkok, Kowloon
Hong Kong

HUNGARY
Kultura
P.O. Box 149
1389 Budapest 62

INDIA
Allied Publishers Private Ltd.
751 Mount Road
Madras - 600 002

Branch offices:
15 J.N. Heredia Marg
Ballard Estate
Bombay - 400 038

13/14 Asaf Ali Road
New Delhi - 110 002

17 Chittaranjan Avenue
Calcutta - 700 072

Jayadeva Hostel Building
5th Main Road Gandhinagar
Bangalore - 560 009

3-5-1129 Kachiguda Cross Road
Hyderabad - 500 027

Prarthana Flats, 2nd Floor
Near Thakore Baug, Navrangpura
Ahmedabad - 380 009

Patiala House
16-A Ashok Marg
Lucknow - 226 001

INDONESIA
Pt. Indira Limited
Jl. Sam Ratulangi 37
P.O. Box 181
Jakarta Pusat

IRELAND
TDC Publishers
12 North Frederick Street
Dublin 1

ITALY
Licosa Commissionaria Sansoni SPA
Via Benedetto Fortini, 120/10
Casella Postale 552
50125 Florence

JAPAN
Eastern Book Service
37-3, Hongo 3-Chome, Bunkyo-ku 113
Tokyo

KENYA
Africa Book Service (E.A.) Ltd.
P.O. Box 45245
Nairobi

KOREA, REPUBLIC OF
Pan Korea Book Corporation
P.O. Box 101, Kwangwhamun
Seoul

KUWAIT
MEMRB Information Services
P.O. Box 5465

MALAYSIA
University of Malaya Cooperative Bookshop, Limited
P.O. Box 1127, Jalan Pantai Baru
Kuala Lumpur

MEXICO
INFOTEC
Apartado Postal 22-860
14060 Tlalpan, Mexico D.F.

MOROCCO
Societe d'Etudes Marketing Marocaine
12 rue Mozart, Bd. d'Anfa
Casablanca

NETHERLANDS
InOr-Publikaties b.v.
P.O. Box 14
7240 BA Lochem

NEW ZEALAND
Hills Library and Information Service
Private Bag
New Market
Auckland

NIGERIA
University Press Limited
Three Crowns Building Jericho
Private Mail Bag 5095
Ibadan

NORWAY
Narvesen Information Center
Bertrand Narvesens vei 2
P.O. Box 6125 Etterstad
N-0602 Oslo 6

OMAN
MEMRB Information Services
P.O. Box 1613, Seeb Airport
Muscat

PAKISTAN
Mirza Book Agency
65, Shahrah-e-Quaid-e-Azam
P.O. Box No. 729
Lahore 3

PERU
Editorial Desarrollo SA
Apartado 3824
Lima

PHILIPPINES
National Book Store
701 Rizal Avenue
P.O. Box 1934
Metro Manila

POLAND
ORPAN
Palac Kultury i Nauki
00-901 Warszawa

PORTUGAL
Livraria Portugal
Rua Do Carmo 70-74
1200 Lisbon

SAUDI ARABIA, QATAR
Jarir Book Store
P.O. Box 3196
Riyadh 11471

MEMRB Information Services
Branch offices:
Al Alsa Street
Al Dahna Center
First Floor
P.O. Box 7188
Riyadh

Haji Abdullah Alireza Building
King Khaled Street
P.O. Box 3969
Damman

33, Mohammed Hassan Awad Street
P.O. Box 5978
Jeddah

SINGAPORE, TAIWAN, MYANMAR, BRUNEI
Information Publications
Private, Ltd.
02-06 1st Fl., Pei-Fu Industrial Bldg.
24 New Industrial Road
Singapore 1953

SOUTH AFRICA, BOTSWANA
For single titles:
Oxford University Press Southern Africa
P.O. Box 1141
Cape Town 8000

For subscription orders:
International Subscription Service
P.O. Box 41095
Craighall
Johannesburg 2024

SPAIN
Mundi-Prensa Libros, S.A.
Castello 37
28001 Madrid

Librería Internacional AEDOS
Consell de Cent, 391
08009 Barcelona

SRI LANKA AND THE MALDIVES
Lake House Bookshop
P.O. Box 244
100, Sir Chittampalam A. Gardiner Mawatha
Colombo 2

SWEDEN
For single titles:
Fritzes Fackboksforetaget
Regeringsgatan 12, Box 16356
S-103 27 Stockholm

For subscription orders:
Wennergren-Williams AB
Box 30004
S-104 25 Stockholm

SWITZERLAND
For single titles:
Librairie Payot
6, rue Grenus
Case postal 381
CH 1211 Geneva 11

For subscription orders:
Librairie Payot
Service des Abonnements
Case postal 3312
CH 1002 Lausanne

TANZANIA
Oxford University Press
P.O. Box 5299
Dar es Salaam

THAILAND
Central Department Store
306 Silom Road
Bangkok

TRINIDAD & TOBAGO, ANTIGUA BARBUDA, BARBADOS, DOMINICA, GRENADA, GUYANA, JAMAICA, MONTSERRAT, ST. KITTS & NEVIS, ST. LUCIA, ST. VINCENT & GRENADINES
Systematics Studies Unit
#9 Watts Street
Curepe
Trinidad, West Indies

TURKEY
Haset Kitapevi, A.S.
Istiklal Caddesi No. 469
Beyoglu
Istanbul

UGANDA
Uganda Bookshop
P.O. Box 7145
Kampala

UNITED ARAB EMIRATES
MEMRB Gulf Co.
P.O. Box 6097
Sharjah

UNITED KINGDOM
Microinfo Ltd.
P.O. Box 3
Alton, Hampshire GU34 2PG
England

URUGUAY
Instituto Nacional del Libro
San Jose 1116
Montevideo

VENEZUELA
Libreria del Este
Aptdo. 60.337
Caracas 1060-A

YUGOSLAVIA
Jugoslovenska Knjiga
P.O. Box 36
Trg Republike
YU-11000 Belgrade